AF522070

TRIBAL MASKS AND MYTHS

TRIBAL MASKS AND MYTHS

Dr. Robin David Tribhuwan
MA., MSc., P.G.D.I.M., Ph.D., Post Doctoral Fellow
Laurence Savelli
MA., Ph.D.

2003

Discovery Publishing House
New Delhi-110002

First Published-2003

ISBN 81-7141-636-5

Published by:

DISCOVERY PUBLISHING HOUSE
4831/24, Ansari Road, Prahlad Street,
Darya Ganj, New Delhi-110002 (India)
Phone: 3279245 • Fax: 91-11-3253475
E-mail:dphtemp@indiatimes.com

Printed at: Tarun Offset Printers, Delhi

Preface

India is perhaps the only country in the world, having over 573 different tribes. According to the 1991 Census the total tribal population of India is 67.8 millions, almost 8.01 per cent to the total populations of the country. Out of the total 573 groups, 75 tribes have been classified as Primitive Tribal Groups. Each tribe is unique and different from each other, because every group has its own cultural and social identity.

Anthropologists and sociologists who have written Monographs on some of the Indian tribes have highlighted interesting and fascinating aspects of tribal cultures in their studies. In this book we have made an effort to unveil the cult of tribal masks in Maharashtra. The focus of the book is on the different types of masks made by the tribals. The process and technique of how these masks are made. The socio-economic status of the mask makers. Festivals associated with mask characters, including the symbolism associated with mask myths. We have also made suggestions regarding how these cults can be preserved and promoted.

This research certainly paves a way for scholars to study other mask cults in the world. We are sure that this book will not only be useful to students and research scholars of Anthropology, Sociology, Art, History, Museology, choreography, Tribal studies, Development planning, but to general readers as well.

Dr. Robin. D. Tribhuwan
MA., MSc., P.G.D.I.M., Ph.D.,
Post Doctoral Fellow
Laurence Savelli
M.A. Ph.D.

Contents

Concepts and Definitions of Masks

INTRODUCTION

The term 'art', has been defined by the Oxford dictionary as a human creative skill or its application. It is a branch of creative activity concerned with production of imaginative designs and expressions. According to Saraf D. N. (1982) "a craft at its finest represents man's need to create an object with mind and hand. Craft is an essentially a skilled solution to a specific need.

Craft and art today, is at the cross-roads and the craftsmen and artisans are in an uneasy situation. The market situation of both artisans and craftsmen has radically changed, while their standards of living has not.

Certain rural and tribal crafts in India have still remained robust as their actual social, ritualistic, ceremonial and cultural functions, are alive. With regards tribal 'art', it would be appropriate to point out, at this juncture that what is 'art' to us urbanites is not 'art' to the tribals. The artefact which is termed as art by us has social, cultural, ritualistic, ceremonial and symbolic meaning associated to, by the tribals.

Thus from an emic point of view tribal artefacts or crafts mean a lot to them. Masks, is no exception to the rule. If we analyse Mask characters of tribals, world over, we would come to a conclusion that every mask represents either a deity, ancestral spirit, totem, mythological character, an event, a person an animal or a bird. Before getting into understanding what types of masks are made by the tribals, the materials they use, their symbolism and so on, let us understand the concept and definition of the term mask.

Definition of Mask

Simply defined, a mask is a form of disguise or an object worn over or in front of the face to hide the identity of a person and by its own features to establish another being.

In other words masks or costumes of a mythological, divine, evil, royal or any other character symbolises a being culturally recognised by the concerned community.

Prevalent since times immemorial in a variety of contexts masks continue to find an important place in the socio-ritual and aesthetic life of the tribals. These masks are made up of clay, paper pulp, metal, wood, bamboo, cowdung, tin and leather as well. Tribals world over use different techniques to make masks.

Types and Techniques of Mask Making

Some techniques of mask making identified by us are as follows:

(a) **Wooden Masks:** For wooden masks the wood of the pangara tree which is light in weight and lends itself easily for carving any shape, is generally preferred. But they also make use of wood from the saag tree (Tectona grandis), although very rerely as this wood is heavy, and not that conducive to carving.

Generally a thick portion of the trunk is loosened and carving is done with an iron chisel and mallet. After carving is done the mask is smoothened by rubbing some coarse material like sand paper on the surface.

(*b*) **Clay Masks:** Here fine and well leviated clay is taken. It is cleaned and sieved so as to remove any coarse and large particles and the clay is soaked in water for 2-3 days. To this is added gum or a sticky juice extracted from the crushed bark of the Mauha tree (Madhuca indica) or that of the bel fruit, so as to increase the sticky nature of the mixture. To this mixture is added cowdung and the entire mixture is kneaded into a fine and supple mixture.

First a rough mask mould is made of wet mud with all its facial features. On this wet mud mould is slapped a thick layer of the clay mixture and the entire thing is allowed to dry in the sun. Next, the mask (of clay) is lifted off the mud mould which crumbles away. Later the facial features are added of highlighted. the mask is given a smooth coating and a fine finish with a sticky juice obtained from the crushed bark of the Mauha tree. (Madhuca indica). After this surface preparation the mask is now ready for further decoration with coloured paper, paint or mirrors.

The manufacture of such a clay mask invovles the preparation of new mud moulds. Each time a new mask in made. Such clay masks usually have a large arch shaped prabhamandala or halo surrounding the mask face.

(*c*) **Bamboo Masks:** These are referred to as that is. These are used to mainly depict a large number of characters in one single mask. Examples of such masks are the Ravana thati, the Pandava thati or the Kaurava thati. In case of the thati a large semi circular or triangular frame around 1-1½ ft in height to 2-3 ft. in length is made of bambo sticks. Over this bamboo frame is fixed either a stiff paper or thin iron sheet. This sheet of iron is covered with coloured paper and decorated with cutouts of various shapes made of bright coloured paper. In case of say a Pandava thati, on the surface are affixed 5 small human figures made of clay mixture. These represent the five pandavas. The lower portion of the thati is fixed on a hollow crown made of bamboo/iron sheet strong enough to balance the weight of the entire thati. This crown is worn on the head.

Similarly in case of a Kaurava thati, more than five small doll like figures are fixed on the thati. The Kauravs are belived to be 100 in number. In case of Ravana thati one comes across both a one headed and a ten headed Ravana thati. In case of the ten headed thati the heads are distributed on either side of the central hollow crown which fits securely on the wearer's head.

Generally two wooden angles are provided with the thatis which enable the wearer of the thati to balance and hold the thati in place while dancing. The wearer of the thati usually paints his face to match with those on the thati.

(d) **Paper Masche Masks:** In recent times, tribal communities have started making paper mache masks wherein two techniques are involved:

(i) Here, a mould is prepared on which layers of soaked news-paper pieces bound to one antoher are slapped. These pieces of news-paper are bound to one another using sticky latex of the bark of tree.

(ii) In this case, paper pulp or paper mache, is prepared by soaking pieces of old newspaper in water for 10-15 days alongwith Methi (Fenugreek) seeds. The two are then ground into a fine pulp which is spread in thick layers over the mask mould made of wet mud. After the two are thoroughly dried the paper mask is taken off the mud mould.

All the masks are further decorated by using colours. Earlier colours were of vegetable origin but now-a-days tribal communities have started using paints that are sold in nearby markets. Generally bright colours are preferred. These colours are red, yellow, green, blue, golden, silver black and white.

(e) **Leather Masks :** These are made of animal skin which has a thick hair cover. The mask is triangular in shape with a pointed head and a broad chin. The face is marked out with white colour and hair from this area is completely shaved off. Eyes are also marked. A triangular shaped nose is fashioned out of skin and it completes the mask.

(f) **Metal Masks:** Among certain tribes we also come across use of metal masks during fairs and festivals. These masks are either made by the tribals themselves or bought from the market. The Agarias of Madhya Pradesh make metal masks, especially of 'Sun God'.

The technique followed is the lost wax technique. A facial form is first made up of clay, on which honey comb wax is used for making the necessary designs or shapes of eyes, ears nose etc. Then, it is dried. Another clay mould is made in which the dried wax mask is inserted. Moulten metal is then put in the mould. The wax inside the mould sticks to the moulten metal thereby contributing to give shape to the mask. If required the Agarias use a chisel and a hammer.

TRIBAL MASKS: AN EMIC VIEW

It is a general notion among educated and urban people that tribal masks are a form of art of the tribal people. Where as in reality, if viewed from an emic perspective, tribal masks are referred to as deities, cosmic beings, demons, royal and princely personalities, animals, spirits, totems and so on. These mythological characters have a meaninful place within the concerned tribal cultures.

Whenever these characters are brought into ritualistic, festive or ceremonical play, the tribals actually believe that these supernatural beings are with people. Hence, they worship these characters with great reverence and respect.

A tribal who wears a mask or costume of a mythological character often fasts; confesses his sins to the concerned mask deity or village god; he may get a vision in which he gets instructions about how he should go about preparing himself to invite the spirits into his body. The action of a mask bearer getting into trance symbolises the entry of a deity in his body.

Thus, to the tribals, maks are mythological, divine, ancestral princely and demonic characters, which are contextually brought into play so as to create a mythological scene. This scene however, remainds the younger generation the significance of knowing myths and preservation of cultural knowledge.

Comparison of Tribal Masks with Hindu Masks

Before getting into discussion on comparison of tribal and Hindu masks, we would like our readers to note that mask cults of tribals living on the plains and those living in inaccessible areas differ. For example Bhil tribe inhabiting in the valleys of Satpuda mountain ranges (North West Maharashtra) have lot of wild animal character masks in their 'Shikari' or hunting dance.

The Bison Horn Madias of Bastar, wear a horn mask during the Holi dance. Thus, tribals living on the mountains, in the valleys and forests have masks of wild animals, jungle spirits, cosmic beings and so on.

Where as tribals living on the plains for several decades, have been interacting with the Hindus and in the process of acculturation have borrowed a number of religious Hindu traits. Tribes such as Mahadev Kolis, Kokna, Warli, Thakars etc. are plain dwelling tribes. They are also small-scale cultivators and have been interacting with the Hindus for ages. We therefore feel that this long term process could have Hinduized these communities to some extent.

Among the tribes of Thane District, in the state of Maharashtra, we have observed Hindu mask characters such as Ganesh, Vishnu, Ram, Laxman, Ravan, Sita, Bhim, Hedumba, Indra and so on. Incorporation of these Hindu traits in tribal festival rituals may have been the master creation of tribal royal families.

For example the province of Jawhar was ruled by the Mukne kings belonging to Mahadev Koli tribe. The kings would encourage cultural activities by sponsoring costumes, food, liquor and other expenses. Ramchandra Bharsat—mask maker from Bharsatmet told us that the king would personally monitor the rehearsals of Bohada festival. The point we are trying to make here is, the members of the royal families were already exposed to urbanization and were Hinduized to a great extent, could have introduced epics such as Mahabharata and Ramayan in the form of drama festival known as Bohada.

Yet another aspect of co-relationship of tribal and Hindu masks is that, we are find Hindus using tribal masks for their rituals. Secondly these are several Hindu masks used in dance forms like Kathakali are not used by the tribals. This whole concept needs to be researched in detail for that matter. There is a need to carryout interdisciplinary reserach on this topic. Keeping in view this background we took up followings aims to study the mask cults of Maharashtra.

Aims of the Study

1. To identify tribal groups that use masks in their cultural rituals.
2. To understand the mask festival of "Bohada", celebrated by the tribals of Thane district, from an emic perspective.
3. To explore the various types of mask characters prevalent among these tribal groups.
4. To unravel the process of making masks.
5. To highlight the status of mask makers.

6. To assess the changes of tribal mask cults have undergone.
7. To unravel myths associated with masks.
8. To suggest strategies to preserve, promote and propagate tribal mask cults.

Significance of the Study

The study is significant both from theoretical and practical perspectives. At the theoretical level it will contribute first of all in unveilling the tribal mask cults of Maharashtra. The concepts and theoretical thoughts presented in the book will pave a way for social scientists as well as students of performing art to develop new theoretical insights. Secondly, this work also presents a methodological approach, which can be used by scholars to study mask cults of other tribal states in India and even tribal communities dwelling in other countries.

At the more practical level, this study intends to impress upon government and non-government organisations associated with tribal culture preservation, that there is a need to pay heed to this declining tribal art of Maharashtra.

Research Methodology

The Need for the Study

India is the only country in the world, which has 573 different tribes, with a population of 67.8 millions. These tribal groups are culturally distinct, as the have culture specific traits. One of the aspects of tribal aesthetics which remained unexplored was the cult of masks. There are hardly any studies on tribal masks and hence, we opted to study this concept keeping in focus tribal Maharashtra. The researchers studied this cult for over.

Setting of the Study

The present study was carried out in Mokhoda and Jawahar tahsils of Thane district in the state of Maharashtra. The villages of Sakur, Bharsatmet, Mokhada, Jawhar, and Dengachimet were studied to understand the cult of tribal masks. Jawhar and Mokhada are thickly populated tribal blocks in Thane district. They are geographically located towards the western side of Bomaby and are 160 kms away from this mega city. Besides this several other tribals groups using masks were studied.

The People

Both in Jawhar and Mokhada some of the major tribes found are Koknas, Warlis, Mahadev Kolis, Thakars, Dhor Kolis, Malhar Kolis, Dublas and Katkaris. Our study however restricted to Koknas, Warlis and the Thakars of the above mentioned.

Tools of Research

The respondents of the study included mask makers, musicians, traditional heads of the village, participant actors in Bohada festival, traders, and tribals of Bharsatmet, Dengachimet, Sakur, Jawhar and Mokhada.

Ten elderly tribals from every village, who have been involved in organising the Bohada festival were slected to gather information on mask cult. Besides, this about 50 participants, seven mask makers, four village heads and at random 50 tribal men and women spectactors from Jawhar and Mokhada were selected to document relevant information. The major tool of research was an interview guide, spearately administered for different type of respondent. This was done to get a holistic view of the mask cult.

The researchers also interviewed dancers belonging to the Bison horn Madias from eastern Maharashtra, Bhils of North Western part and other tribal groups using masks for rituals. These interviews were taken by the authors. Besides using interview guide, case study method was also adepted to gather relevant information on the mask makers. Thus, both interview guide and case study methods were the major tools of research.

Analysis

Since the data collected on mask cults of tribals was qualitative in nature, it was analysed manually.

Chapter Scheme

The data has been presented in Six chapters namely:

(i) Concepts and Definitions of Masks

(ii) Research Methodology

(iii) Tribal villages, people and the Mask Makers

(iv) Bohada: The Mask Festival of Bharsatmet

(v) Bohoda: As interpreted by non-Tribals.

(vi) Summary and Conclusions.

Tribal Villages, People and Mask Makers

An Introduction to the Tribes of Maharashtra

The State of Maharashtra ranks second as regards tribal population size in the country. There are 47 tribal communities an Maharashtra, with a population of 73.18 lakhs, amounting to 9.27 per cent to the total population of the state. Grographically these tribal groups are found in west, northwest and eastern parts of Maharashtra.

Since the nature of the research problem revolved around understanding tribal masks, we chose to work among the western tribes of Maharashtra. Thane district, principally is a prominent tribal district having mask cults, were selected to study the mask cult.

As mentioned earlier five villages namely:

1. Bharasatmet village in Jawahar tahsil;
2. Ramkhind hamlet of Sakur village in Jawhar Tahsil;
3. Dengachimet village in Jawhar tahsil;
4. Jawhar tahsil;
5. Mokhada tahsil.

All these villages are far away from main cities and towns and are underdeveloped. The tribal concerntration in these villages are very high, though in Jawhar and Mokhada have non-tribals as well. Table 3.1 gives details about tribal groups found in the above mentioned villages.

Table 3.1
Tribes Inhabiting in Sample Villages

S. No.	Villages	Tribe Inhabiting
1.	Ramkhind Hamlet of Sakuar village	1. Warli 2. Kokna 3. Dhor Koli
2.	Bharsatmet	1. Kokna 2. Few Warlis
3.	Denganchimet	1. Kokna 2. Few Warlis
4.	Jawhar	1. Mahadev Kolis 2. Warlis 3. Thakars 4. Katkaris 5. Koknas 6. Dhor Kolis 7. Malhar Kolis
5.	Mokhada	1. Kokna 2. Warlis 3. Thakars 4. Mahadev Kolis

Before getting into understanding the mask makers and their techniques of making masks. Let us glance briefly at the ethnographic background of the Koknas, Thakars, Mahade Koli, Dhorkoli Malhar Koli, Katkari and Warlis.

Brief Background of Tribes Under Study

Major tribes found in Thane district are:

Thakars, Koknas, Mahadey Kolis, Malhar Kolis, Dhor Kolis, Dublas, Katkaris and Warlis. Each tribe has its unique cultural trait that makes them different from each other. However all of them participate in Mask Festival.

Mask Makers

Out of the 47 tribes only 8-10 tribes namely Koknas, Warlis, Bhils, Madias, Thakars, Mahadev Kolis, Dhor Kolis, Malhar Kolis, Katkaris, and Korkus are known for making masks. These masks are of different materials such as wood, paper masche, cowdung, bamboo, clay and even metal. Prominent among all the tribal mask makers are Ramchandra Bharsat, from Bharsatmet village and Dharma Rama Kadu from Ramkhind hamlet of Sakur village, in Jawhar tahsil of Thane district. These two-have made all types of masks except the metal ones. Both Ramchandra and Dharma devoted their lives for mask making and have become very popular in Jawhar and Maharashtra as well.

CASE STUDY NO. 1

A. Personal Information

Name	—	Dharma Rama Kadu
Age	—	68
Sex	—	Male
Tribe	—	Member of a Warli Tribe
Address	—	Ramkhind hamlet, Sakur village, Jawhar Tahsil, Thane District, (M.S.), India.
Marital Status	—	Married
Land Holding	—	2 acres

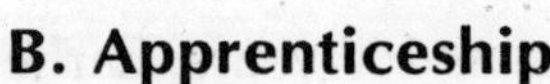

B. Apprenticeship

Dharma Kadu started his career as a mask maker at the age of 7, when he lived with his father in Bharsatmet village. His father passed away, when Dharma was 8 years old. From then on, he was taken care of by Pandharinath Sonar, the famous mask maker of Jawhar who lived 100 years ago.

Dharma used to work in Pandharinath's farm and house, for which he would get food. While working with Pandharinath, Dharma slowly but surely developed interest in mask making. He started helping Pandharinath with mask making. Within 10 years he mastered the art of mask making. When he was 18 years old, he married a Warli girl from Bharsatmet and then moved to Ramkhind, wherein he settled.

He started growing rice for his sustainance. During off seasons of cultivation, i.e. from November to March, Dharma started making masks and selling them to the tribals around his village. He was supported by his villagers and Mr. Kirkira the village head. Dharma would make masks of clay, wood, bamboo and paper masche. From the tribals he would take food grains, whereas from the non-tribals he would receive money.

He was spotted by number of government and non-government organisations as an artist. He would be called to cities for exhibitions. Museums invited him to make masks. Well this is how he became popular. Dharma must have earned 30 to 40 thousand rupees in his life time by selling masks. He was motivated by Dr. Robin. D. Tribhuwan, an Anthropologist and Social Worker, to pass on the art of mask making to his sons. Dharma did train his two sons. The project officer, of Jawhar sponsored Dharma to teach 10 other tribals this art. This is how Dr. Robin contributed in preserving this art. Dharma died in the month of August, 2001. He is survived by three sons. His contribution will certainly be remembered.

Traditional Process of Mask Making

On enquiring the traditional method of mask making Dharma said traditionally mask making was restricted to clay, cowdung, wood and leather masks. The art of paper masche mask is as old as 100 years. Earlier we would make masks of either clay, cowdung, or mixture of both and wooden masks of course. He said earlier natural colours extracted from leaves, petals of flowers and roots of certain herbs were used as colours for painting the masks.

In the early 1900 Pandharinath Bharsat, popularly known as sonar, started experimenting with masks of tree barks and later on paper masche. The process of making paper masche as followed by late Pandharinath Bharsat the teacher of Dharma Kadu is as follows:

1. Prepare a oval clay structure from black smooth clay;
2. Soak soft bark and news papers, or card boards in the latex of Mauha tree (Madhuca indica). The latex is sticky;
3. Mix these ingradients with methi seed power;
4. Add gum to the mixture;
5. Then, paper pulp, is put on the clay base and depending on the shape he wants he moulds the masche accordingly and makes a mask;
6. This mask is then dried in the sun for a week;
7. The dried mask is then painted using leaf, flower, and bark colours;
8. They would be then dried.

Dhama Rama Kadu invented another method to mix the paper pulp. He found a tree called cherry. The bark of this tree is removed and soaked in a small pond for 3 to 4 weeks. The mixture becomes very stick. He would then add paper or card board to it and mix it. This masche would then be put on the dry clay base to give it a form.

Well, the process for making wooden masks is different. There are only two phases in this. One is carving a mask from a block of wood

and secondly painting it. Dharma Kadu says that he may have made over 1000 masks using the traditional colours and method.

Modern Method of Preparing Masks

There has not been much change in the traditional method of mask making, except that synthetic paint is being used for painting the masks. Secondly a lot of coloured paper is also being used by mask makers to decorate the masks, especially bamboo masks.

How Does he Look at Himself Now?

Dharma Kadu is very happy and proud of himself as an artist. Through out his life he might have made ever 2000 masks for tribals, museums, foreigners, and urbanities interested in tribal art. He feels that an artist like him should be given pension, every month as an incentive. He says the Tribal Development Department (Sarkar) should give him at least 300 Rs. per month as a pension. I am old now, and have a old wife as well. We are in need of money. He has taught this art to 14 tribals including his sons. Dharma died in August, 2001. He will Certainly be remembered by the musuems for which he had mode masks.

CASE STUDY NO. 2

A. Personal Information

Name	—	Ramchandra Pandharinath Bharsat
Age	—	60
Sex	--	Male
Tribe	—	Kokna,
Address	—	At post Bharsatmet, Jawhar Tahsil, Thane District, Maharashtra, India;
Marital Status	—	Married, without children
Land Holding	—	8 acres of land.

B. Apprenticeship

After studying Ramchandra's skill as a mask maker for nearly three years, we came to a conclusion that he is the best mask maker in the State of Maharashtra. He is truely an artisan who applies his mind, invents new methods and skills, and produces the best mask. He received training from his father since the age of 4. His father not only taught him to make masks, but also mental notifs and statues. Most tribals would come to pandharinath for making mental motifs and Statues. These figures would be of ancestral memorials or clan gods and goddesses. Infact pandharinath as well as Ramchandra are the only tribals in the state who make masks as well as copper; brass and silver motifs, manually. they never used moulds to make the motifs.

Ramchandra first received his lesson when he was 4 years old. His father, would make him sit next to him and would teach him how to make metal motifs and masks as well. Many times Ramchandra was severely beaten for not learning the art.

C. Process of Making Masks

Ramchandra mostly used the techniques of making masks which were taught to him by Pandharinath, his father. Except that Ramchandra mastered the art of using best synthetic paints and decorations. His sense of colour combinations is too good.

D. His Contribution to Preservation

As a mask maker Ramchandra no doubt preserved the techniques of mask making, but interestingly he is the only artist who took active part in organising the Bohada Festival of mask is his village. He has been into it for nearly 40 years. He is respected in his village for this.

E. His View as an Artist

As a unique mask maker and a metal craftsman Ramchandra is proud that he is the only artist of his quality in the state of Maharashtra. He

has never trusted people who organised exhibitions. He was cheated by a government curator during one exhibition. From then on he did not participate in exhibitions. He gets enough money to sustain himself in the vilalge. He has a small grocery shop, agricultural land and his business of making metal motifs, paper masche and wooden masks.

Both Ramchandra and his wife are very upset that they do not have a child, to pass on the art to. He has motivated by Dr. Robin Tribhuwan to pass on the knowledge and art to his brother's son. Ramchandra was never interested in teaching any one else.

CASE STUDY NO. 3

A. Personal Information

Name	—	Subhash Dharma Kadu
Age	—	24
Sex	—	Male
Tribe	—	Warli
Education	—	VIIth grade
Address	—	Ramkhind Hamlet, Sakur Village, Jawhar, Thane District
Marital Status	—	Married
Land Holding	—	One acre

B. Uniqueness of Subhash

Subhash has learnt the art of mask making from his father Dharma Kadu. He uses all the tchniques taught to him by his father. What is unique about Subhash is that, he has started making Hindu masks as per the demands of Hindu people. He has also started making paper masche

toys of rabbit, tortoise, monkeys etc. These new innovations have been adopted by Subhash because of his frequent visits to Bombay to sell his masks.

In fact every week he goes with his brother to Bomaby to a play called Kalaghoda and sells masks on footpath. The Bombay people purchase his art. He also visits art institutions and trains urban children the art of making masks. That is why he is different.

His View Towards Art

Subhash is grateful to his father for the knowledge he has passed on to him. He wishes to programme in life as an artist.

CASE STUDY NO.4

A. Personal Information

Name	—	Krishna Navsu Raut
Age	—	45
Tribe	—	Kokna
Education	—	Illiterate
Address	—	Peth Tahsil, Nasik District, Maharashtra State
Marital Status	—	Married
Land Holding	—	5 acres

B. Apprenticeship

Learnt the art of making only wooden masks and statues from his father. He started his career as a wooden mask maker at the age of 15. He has been supplying masks to tribals in Nasik and Thane as well.

C. Uniqueness of Krishna

His uniqueness lies in making only wooden masks and more importantly wooden statues. He has also participated in several exhibitions organised by government and non-government organisations.

Along with his father, he has carved several stutues of both tribal and Hindu deities. Earlier they would get foodgrains for their services. Now-a-days money is preferred.

View Towards Art

He says this art has given him a platform to survive. It is like a ray of hope for him. Secondly, he belives that god-Sun, gives him power to create different images of gods. He feels satisfied with the same.

Reflections on the Mask Makers

As compared to the 73.18 lakh population of tribals in Maharashtra, there are only 20 to 30 mask makers in Thane and Nasik Districts who have been making masks to keep the flame of Bohada alive. It is high time for government and N.GO's to tkae up a survey of tribal artisans so as to identify their artistic potentical and finally encourage them to preserve, promote and propagate the same.

Secondly, as aptly revealed by Dharma Kadu, none of them do not get any financial incentive from the government, especially when they retire or become old for that matter. Efforts should be made to provide them nutritional, medical and financial help through I.T.D.P's.

Bohada: The Mask Festival of Bharsatmet

Where is Bharsatmet?

Bharsatmet village is located about 16 Kms away from Jawahar tahsil, of Thane district, in Maharashtra State India. The village is predominently inhabited by the Koknas with few Warli houses. The total population of Bharsatmet is 1600, as per 1991, census.

This village is one of the popular villages known for "Bohada"—the mask festival. People from Nasik, Bombay, Gujarat, Sylvasa, Daman etc. come to see this tribal festival. Primary data collected from the villagers of Bharsatmet and Ramachandra Bharsat—the master mask maker, revealed that this tradition is as old as the village. They were however, able to take back their memory 300 years ago. Today there is a mask made out of wood by the grandfather of Ramachandra. This mask character is called "Ghuba Devi" and is 200 years old.

Ramachandra's forefathers were mask and copper motif makers. Infact it would be appropriate to make a statement that Ramachandra is the best mask maker in tribal Maharashtra and is among the few craftsman who makes copper, alluminium and brass motifs without using moulds.

He along with the village head's family have been responsible to preserve and promote this traditional art. He takes active interest in organizing the Bohada festival, which takes place for three days.

Organisers of Bohada Festival

As mentioned earlier the key role to organise the Bohada festival is played by Ramachandra the mask maker, the village head and at least 30 village elders. These 30 village elders represent those families which keep mask characters at home, maintain and preserve them. They are given the responsibility of taking care of these masks. Each family owns a mask. This mask is covered in a sari and safely kept on the loft of their house. It is removed only 10 to 15 days before the festival, in case of re-painting or decorating the same. These mask owners pay Rs. 100-150 to the organising committee. This committee works on the preparation and management of the festival.

Preparation Phase

Bohada festival usually occurs after holi. When we attended this festival it was on 5th, 6th and 7th of May 2000. We observed all the phases of the festival.

A. Fund Raising by the Villagers

Every house hold of Bharsatmet is concerned about fund raising. As mentioned earlier all the families owning a mask pays Rs. 100-150/- per family, towards the organisational fund. Besides this, other families donate between Rs. 10-50. The Warlis who have been converted to 'Malkari' cult, do not pay anything. Malkaris are people who refrain from drinking, eating non-vegetarian food and narcotics. They have also taken up worshipping hindu deities and hence do not participate in the festival. On an average the villagers of Bharsatmet are able to collect Rs. 5000 to 8000/- every year, on their own.

B. Contribution by Traders

Since tribals and non-tribals from far and near attend the festival, traders also come to sell their goods. The organising committee receives Rs. 50 to 150 depending on what kind of goods are sold by the trader. This money is considered as tax. The villagers called it "Dār Patti".

C. Contribution by the Visitors

Visitors who come to watch the festival from other villages are approached to contribute voluntarily for the festival. We contributed Rs. 500/- during the year 1999.

D. Purchasing Material

Once an amount of Rs. 10 to 15 thousand is gathered then the members of the organising committee discuss on purchasing material and also payment of people who contirbute to the making of the festival. Individuals are send to buy the material, summon musicians, decoration contractor etc.

E. Expenditure

Major expense of the festival can be categorised under following budget heads.

- *(i)* Paint, brushes, colour paper, bamboo, etc. for renovating masks;
- *(ii)* Painting and cleaning the Hanuman temple in the village;
- *(iii)* Purchasing coconuts and other items of puja;
- *(iv)* Honorarium of Katkari/Mahar musicians. Kathkari is another tribe, while Mahars are a backward caste community, traditionally assigned to play music for Bohada processions;
- *(v)* Expense in lighting and decorating the streets of the village;

Khanderao—A Male Deity.

Vishnu—A Male Deity.

A Kokna Man with Mask of Vishnu.

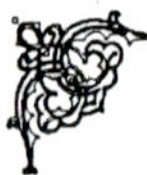

Brahma Dev—Creator.

Kalbhairi—A Female Deity.

Narsiha—A Male Deity.

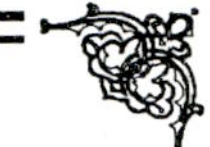

Ghubadevi—A Female Deity.
A Wooden Mask Which 200 Years Old.

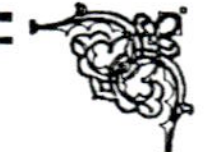

Mhaisasur—A Male Demon.

Indradev—A Male Deity.

Krishna—A Male Deity.

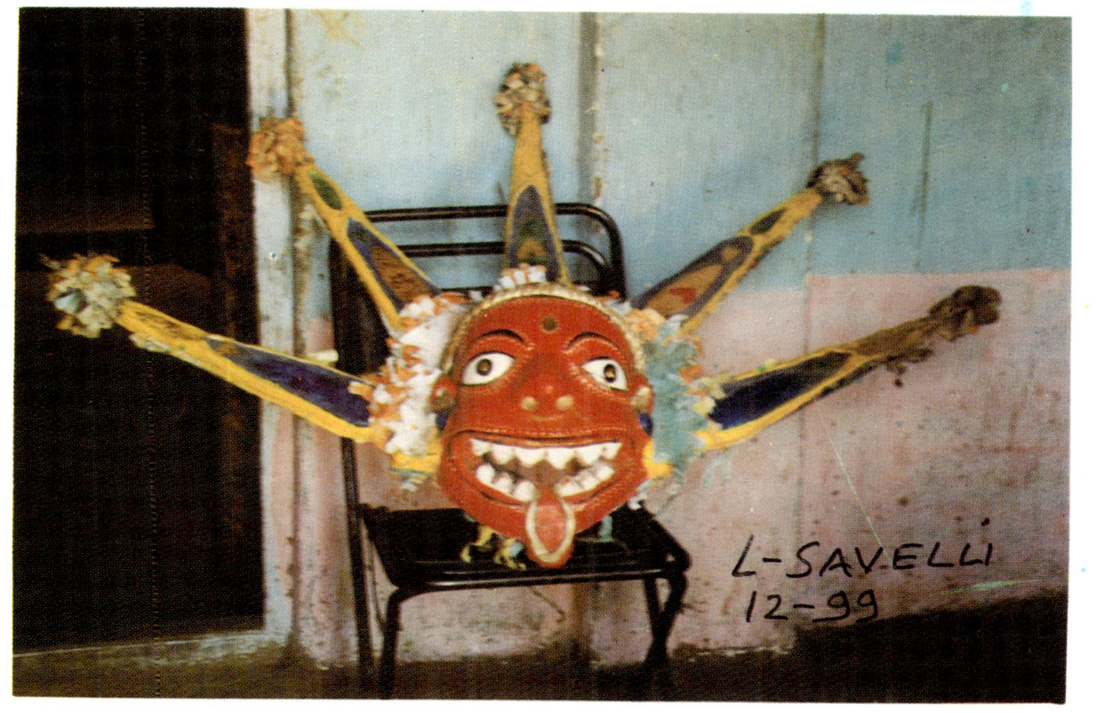

Hedumba—A Female Demon, Sister of Ravana.

Raktadevi—Goddess who Requires Blood.

Dhavloba—A Male Deity.

Ramtati—A Bamboo Mask with four Characters from left Sita, Ram, Laxman and Hanuman.

Jagdamba—An Incarnation of Parvati.
A Female Deity.

Chandradev: Moon God.

Satvai: Mother Earth.

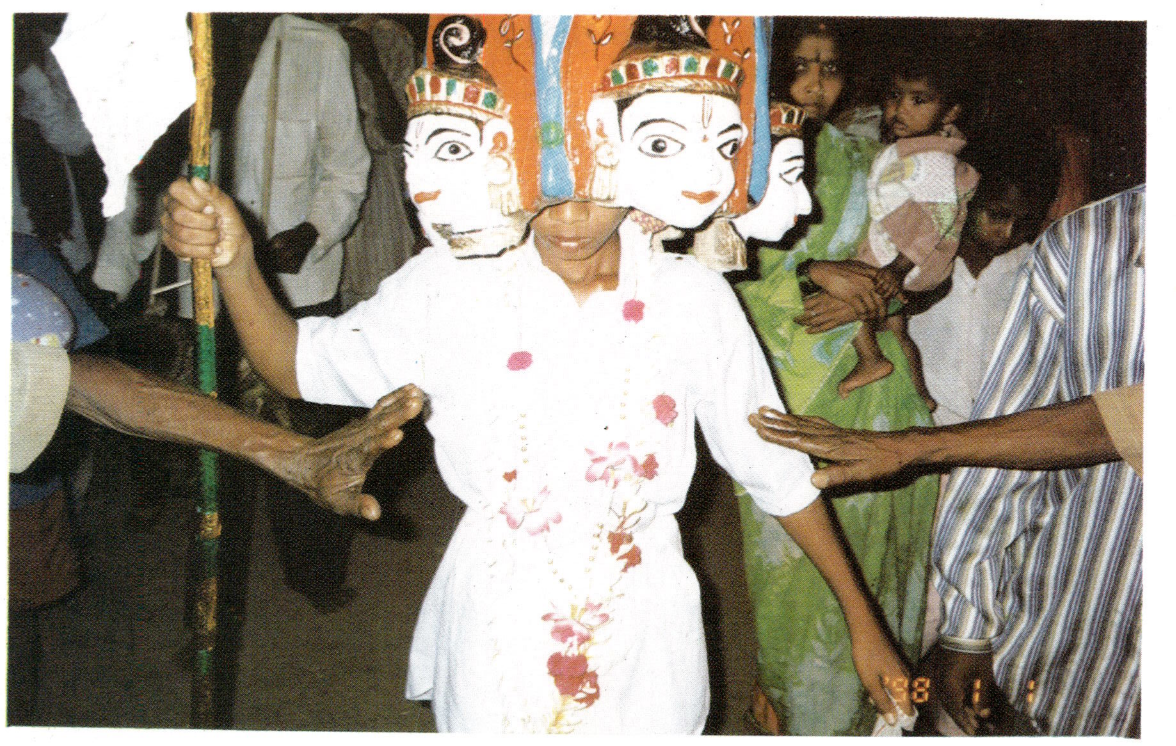

Trimurti—Three Demon.

Ganesh—Male Deity.

Bibisen—Male Demon.

Shanker with Ganga in his Hair.

Tribals Grow Seeds of Rice in a Basket for 7 days and then offer the same to the Village Goddess. Every Family Grows this Basket and on the first eve of Bohada there Baskets are Offered to the Goddess.

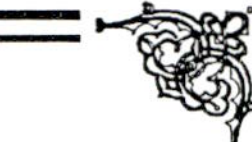

Goddess of Bharsatmet Village.

From Left Dr. Robin Tribhuwan with Ramchandra and his Wife.

Left Raja Mahendra Singh Mukne the 20th Tribal King of Jawhar Being Greeted by Krushna Dingere—the Tailor.

First Procession is of the Village Headman.

First Lady Worshipping Hanuman.

Krishna in a Procession.

Bamboo Mask of Ravana— The Male Demon.

Kaurav Tati—Bamboo Mask Depicting Kauravas

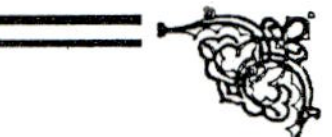

Kalbhairi— The Female Goddess in Procession.

Bamboo Mask Depicting Rama, Laxman, Sita, and Hanuman.

Rakta Devi is Procession.

Khanderao in Procession.

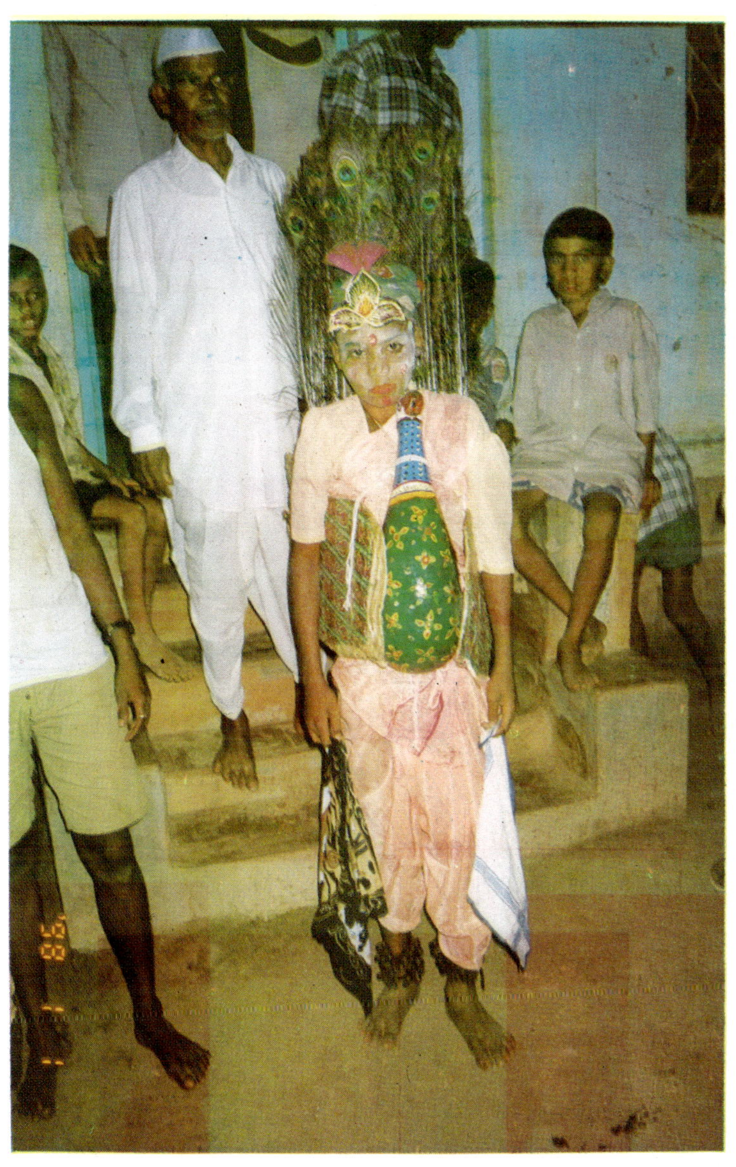

Saraswati— A Female Deity.

Clowns— Men Dress as Women to Make Fun.

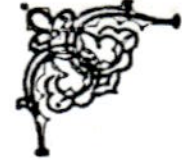

Bhim Ready to Fight with Bakasur.

Satvai— Mother Goddess.

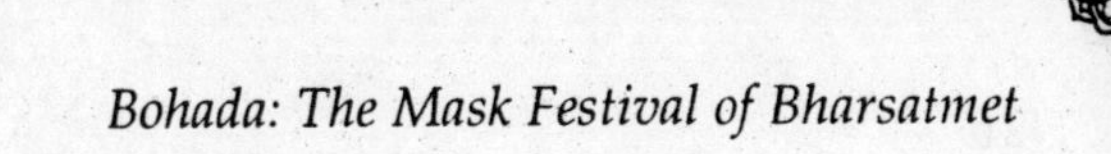

(vi) Expense on alcohol;

(vii) Expense for Kerosine and latterns;

(viii) Food expenditure;

(xi) Costumes purchase;

(x) Miscellaneous expenses.

F. Painting Masks

Responsibility of painting, decorating the masks is fully bestowed upon Ramachandra—the chief mask maker. He starts his buisness one month before the festival.

G. Assigning Places to Traders

Asigning places to vendors and hawkers depends on first come first served basis. Traders come one month in advance and book their places. Thus, money is collected one month in advance from the traders.

H. Rehearsal of Participant Actors (Mask Characters)

It is the responsibility of the village head and Ramachandra to supervise the rehearsal sessions of Bohada. Every mask owner comes for the practice or sends his son. These guys are asked to enact the whole scene and their individual roles during practice sessions.

I. Village Head: The Co-ordinator

Luxman Pandu Bharsat, the traditional head of Bharsatmet pours in his entire experience and potential to make the festival a success. He co-ordinates, monitors, and checks every activity of the festival.

J. Role of Ramachandra

Ramachandra Bharsat the chief mask maker and a master craftsman

is the soul of the festival. He dedicates his time, talent and energy without charging a single peny to make the festival a success.

K. Co-operation of the Villagers

Not to forget the honest and sincere efforts put in by the villagers of Bharsatmet. Their active participation too contributes to the success of the festival.

Bohada Festival in Action

First signs of Bohada in Bharsatmet are scenes of tribals and non-tribals in groups and families moving towards Bharsatmet. On 5th of May 1999, we witnessed tribals walking towards this historic village to participate in the festival. People seemed relaxed and happy as they marched on.

As they enter the village there is place to park their bullock-carts outisde the village. We also witnessed a number of two-wheelers parked outside. Maximum tribals had walked all the way to the village, while some came in buses, trucks, tractors, and rikshaws.

(a) Scene in the Village

As soon as you enter the village, you witness crowdedness. People take their positions on the countryards. Few stand, while most sit. They wait for the festival to begin. One also gets to see traders shouting to attract the attention of buyers. Children make noise, run around, shout and play. The main street of Bharsatmet is just crowded. By six, in the evening they put on the lights.

(b) Village Head Welcomes the Musicians

Musicians who are hired for three nights are welcomed by the head. They are offered liquor, bidis (cigars) and tobacco. By eight in the night after their dinner musicians start tunning their instruments. By now Bharsatmet has over 10,000 people gathered to witness the festival.

(c) Headman's Party Comes Out in a Procession

By the time it is 9 in the night, the first event of the festival starts with musicians playing durms and clarenets. There are two drummers playing (Sambulas) two triangular sets of drums and two tribal musicians play clarenet, while one exclusively plays a base clarenet.

While the music is on the "Pahily Pati"—the first procession starts. It is led by the musicians from the headman's house to the Hanuman temple. The members include village head, his wife, Rama Chandra, his wife and other family members of village head.

The women folk carry 'aarti' and coconuts in plate and basket. The first lady of the village, i.e. the head's wife offers a puja to Hanuman—the monkey god. She is followed by other women who offer 'aarti' to Hanuman. This is followed by breaking of coconuts starting off with the village head, followed by Ramachandra and then other male members of the headman's family. Once this in done, mask characters are brought in procession from the village head's house uptil the temple of Hanuman. Every mask is worn by the owner or his son and is accompanied by the musicians in a procession.

Mask Characters

Tribals of Jawhar, Mokhada and Peth tahsils of Thane and Nasik districts have revealed that there are as many as 52 characters of Bohada festival. However, when actually observed in Bharsat met—a village of the Kokna tribe, it was discovered that there are 30 traditional mask characters, possessed by 30 clans. These 30 characters are:

1. Naran dev
2. Masa or Fish
3. Sarjadevi or Saraswati—Peocock
4. Ganapati—or Ganesh
5. Mahadev
6. Indradev
7. Khanderao

(Contd... .)

8. Kaloba
9. Niloba
10. Bhairoba
11. Kalbhairi
12. Ram Tati
13. Kaurav Tati
14. Hedumba
15. Mhaisasur
16. Bakasur
17. Ravan
18. Vishnudev
19. Chanddev
20. Suryadev
21. Bhim-Bakasur
22. Raktadevi
23. Ghubadevi
24. Agnidev
25. Londhya
26. Narsihva
27. Satwai
28. Kumbha Karma—Brother of Ravan
29. Bibisan—Brother of Ravan
30. Krishna

Other Characters (Used in Bohadas by the Warlis, Thakars, Kokna etc.)

31. Charnin	—	a female herder
32. Tōp	—	a man with a cap
33. Balantin	—	new mother
34. Gavalani	—	a female herders
35. Garud	—	Eagle
36. Waghoba	—	Tiger
37. Sinhva	—	Lion

(Contd… .)

38. Kasav	—	Tortoise
39. Dait	—	a male demon
40. Bhil Tati	—	A mask representing-Bhils
41. Ekadas	—	one headed mask
42. Duvadas	—	Two headed masks
43. Zakati Tati	—	small bamboo mask
44. Vithoba	—	hindu male god
45. Rukhmai	—	hindu female goddess
46. Vetal	—	An evil forest spirit
47. Gajasur	—	long faced Ganesh
48. Ghoda	—	Horse
49. Evana	—	mythological character
50. Dhavloba	—	Mask with white face
51. Maha Laxmi	—	female goddess
52. Shivaji Maharaj	—	a Maratha king

Bohada festival celebrated in Bharsatmet village in Jawhar block of Thane district displayed 30 characters. Each mask character is enacted by a male member of a family. For instance the character of Satvai—the goddess of fertility is enacted by Chandrakant Govanda. Earlier his father, grandfather and great grandfather enacted the same. This family has to permanently take care of that mask. Every year it has to be decorated and maintained by the same family. During Bohada festival people of Bharsatmet send each character in a sequence. These are as follows:

SEQUENCE OF MASK CHARACTERS DISPLAYED IN BHARSATMET

S. No.	Mask Character		Name of the Actor
1.	Naradmuni	— —	Yashwant Pawar
2.	Saraswati	— —	Narayan Barsat
3.	Ganpati	— —	Ganesh Gavli
4.	Maruti	— —	Shashi Kant Barsat
5.	Satvai	— —	Chandrakant Govanda
6.	Bhim and Bakasur	— —	Lahu Bhusar
7.	Kalbhairi	— —	Namdev Pawar
8.	Trimurti	— —	Hari Raghu Dalvi
9.	Vishnudev	— —	Subhash Dalvi
10.	Kaurav Thati	— —	Jayant Shanker Barsat
11.	Indra dev	— —	Bhasker Khirari
12.	Ramtati*	— —	Devram Bhusar
13.	Brahma dev	— —	Vijay Dalvi
14.	Raktadevi	— —	Suresh Maule
15.	Agnidev	— —	Ramchandra Barsat
16.	Ṡri Krishna	— —	Ramchandra Barsat
17.	Kaloba	— —	Bhaurao Bhole
18.	Khanderao	— —	Luxman Barsat

(Contd... .)

**Character No. 12*

Ram Thati has three characters namely Ram, Laxman and Sita.

19.	Hedumba	—	—	Ganpat Gavit
20.	Vetal	—	—	Sadashiv Barsat
21.	Narsivha	—	—	Vasant Raghu Dalvi
22.	Ravan	—	—	Ram Pawar
23.	Dait	—	—	Dasrat Bharsat
24.	Jagdamba	—	—	Magan Ramu Barsat
25.	Mhashasur	—	—	Govind Raju Pawar
26.	Londhya	—	—	Bhauram Parshuram Maule

Evil or Demonic Characters

1. *Bhim Bakasur*—Bakasur or a demon popularly known as 'Rakshas' who fought with "Bhima" is named as Bhim Bakasur.
2. *Ravan*—The demon who lived in Lanka', currently known as a Sri Lanka situated, towards the south of India. Ravan had ten heads. He fought with Ram and Laxman, when they were in exile for 14 years. Ravan is said to have captured 'Sita' i.e. Rama's wife, hence the fight, took place.
3. *Hedumba*—is believed to be the sister of Ravana.
4. *Narsivha*—is yet another male demon.
5. *Dait*—a male demon, belongs to the family of demons.
6. *Vetal*—a male forest spirit, that usually moves in the thick woods.
7. *Mhashasur*—a male demon who is killed by Jagdamba on the last day of the "Bohada" festival.
8. *Londhya*—After Mhashasur the dreadful demon is killed, another male evil demon comes out of his stamoch. He is known as Londhya.

Good or Holy Mask Characters

1. *Narad muni:* A form of Brahmans who act like brahmans.

2. *Saraswati:* Sits on the peacock. Peacock to the tribals is "Hirva" a clan deity. Here again it is a fusion of Hindu and tribal deities. The dance shows more action of peacock flying than the goddess.

3. *Ganpati:* The son of Shiva and Parvati is taken in a procession.

4. *Maruti:* The monkey god and a devottee of Ram.

5. *Satvai:* Mother earth who writes the fortune and life span of every human being. That is why whenever a child is born, on the fifth day, it is offered to Satvai for her to decide his life span. Most tribals in Maharashtra worship Satvai on the fifth day after the child is born. They place a child in a basket. A basket is half hemisphere or half part of mother earth in this situation. This basket is a symbol of earth's womb called 'oti'. So they thank the womb of mother earth who is productive and fertile for making the new mother fertile.

6. *Bhim and Bakasur*: Bhim is one of the characters in Mahabharata. He is one of the brother of Panch Pandavas. Where as Bakasur is a demon. Bhim fights with Bakasur in the play and defeats him.

7. *Kalbhairi:* Kalbhairi is a black faced mask with a green crown. He is suppose to be protecting tribals from snakes. If someone is bitten by a snake, ash is applied on the forehead of the patient in the name of Kalbhairi. This socio-ritualistic treatment has an impact on the psyche of the patient. It helps him to come out of the fear that he is going to die.

8. *Trimurti:* As the name suggests "trimurti" is a three faced god, none other than Brahma, Vishnu and Mahesh.

9. *Vishnu Dev:* One of the characters of the trinity, i.e. Vishnu is displayed separately by the Kokanas of Bharsatmet.

10. *Kaurav Thati:* Kavravs are 100 brothers, all characters from the Hindu epic Mahabharata. The Kokanas of Bharstmet make either 10 or 100 small masks on a bamboo mat and is displayed during the Bohada festival. This is done to recreate the mythological scene from Mahabharata.

11. *Indra Dev:* The God of fire, is shown with yellowish or light pink face.

12. *Ramtati*: A bamboo mat on which figures of Ram, Laxman and Sita are displayed is called Ram tati. In Bharsatmet Koknas display two types of thee characters.

    1. *Ram tati*: the Bamboo mat with three statues of Ram, Laxman and Sita, the heros of Ramayan epic.

    2. The living characters of Ram, Laxman and Sita enacted by the Koknas. Three men dress up like Ram, Laxman and Sita and act while they are taken on the streets of Bharsat. The procession is lead by the musicians.

13. *Brahmadev*: One of the characters from Trimurti, is Brahma—the creator.

14. *Rakta Devi*: Rakta refers to blood, and Devi to godess. Tribals worship the goddess who requires animal sacrifice.

15. *Agnidev*: Agni refers to fire, hence the god of fire. The tribals associate him with sun, and not Indra Dev.

16. *Sri Krishna:* Is the famous hero of Mahabharata of the Hindu epic. He is usually enacted by a small boy, who wears the mask of Krishna and walks in the procession.

17. *Kaloba:* The black faced mask is yet another clan deity of the Kokna.

18. *Khanderao:* Yet another Hindu deity, mostly worshipped by the people from middle and lower caste groups.

19. *Jagdamba:* Jagdamba or 'Ambadevi' is the most important mask character of "Bohada festival". Its procession is taken out on the third day at 11° clock. People offer her (mask character) coconut, poultry birds, goats etc. The term "Amba" refers to mango. One of the respondents said that since her festival occurs at the time of mango season, she may have got the name "Amba". All the tribals, however say she is the symbol of mother earth—the goddess of fertility, good grains, trees, vegetation, fruits, water, life. She is considered to be their sustainer. They say we are able to survive because of "Jagdamba".

The Non-tribals in the vicinity however associate her with-Kali, who kills Mahishasur—a demon on the Dasera festival. The Koknas however enact the scene of "Amba devi" killing "Mahishasur—a wild buffallo mask bearer" in the play. We feel 'Amba devi' is a cyncritized symbol of tribal and Hindu myths.

The last character in the play is Londhya—a demon, who is given birth to after the death of Mahishasur.

Bharsatmet people also have other mask characters such as "Ghuba Devi"—the goddess with bulging cheeks. This mask is a wodden mask, nearly 200 years old. This was made by Ramchandra's great grandfather. The people of Bharsatmet, who belongs to the Kokna community worship all the masks with aspect and reverence. They believe that these masks are representatives of actual gods and goddesses. It is like all the gods are with them, to protect them from disasters and other calamities.

Another interesting aspect of the Bohada Masks of Bharsatmet is that all these masks are made by one family of artisans, i.e. Ramchandra Pandharinath Bharsat. Other than the above mentioned 30 masks, Koknas of Bharsatmet do not display other characters.

Other Mask Characters

Bohada is also celebrated by tribals in other parts of Thane and Nasik. These places are Mokhada, Dahanu and Jawhar in Thane and Peth and Surgana in Nasik. Different villages display different mask characters. Some of the other mask characters not discussed in the book are:

1. *Charnin*—A female forest spirit and care taker of the cattle. She is the goddess of tribal cow boys. She protects the cattle from tigers and other wild animals;

2. *Tōp*—is yet another character of a man, wearing a long cap. Top is another word for cap;

3. *Balatin*—the goddess who presides over the process of delivery. She ensures safe delivery of a new born;

4. *Gavalani*—are seven planetary spirits, believed to be sisters of mother earth. They are spinsters. They visit a human body in the form of hot air, this erupts skins and causes chicken pox, measles boils and Visitation of Gavalani is considered to be auspicious;

5. *Garud*—Is the eagle, referred in Hindu myths as a vihicle of gods.

6. *Waghoba*—The famous tiger god of the tribes in western Maharashtra. The Warlis and Thakars have him as a village god;

7. *Sinhva*—The Lion god. His maks is made and worshipped during Bohada;

8. *Kasav*—Tortoise god is suppose to be a clan deity. It is has medicinal properties;

9. *Dait:* Is a demon from the South direction.

10. *Bhil Thati*—A Bamboo mat on which figures of Bhil tribals are fixed. This mat is taken in procession during 'Bohada'. Bhils

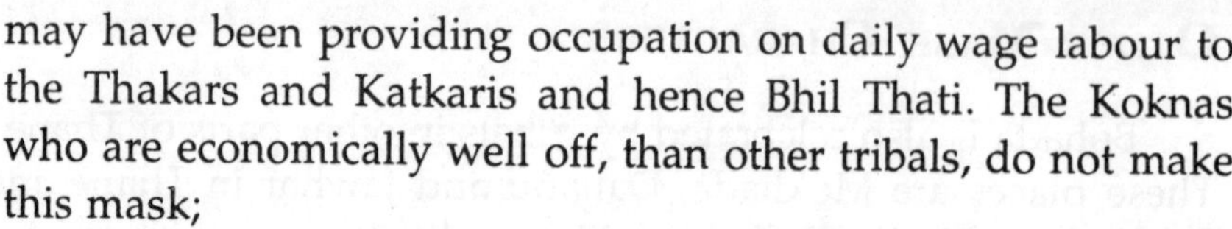

may have been providing occupation on daily wage labour to the Thakars and Katkaris and hence Bhil Thati. The Koknas who are economically well off, than other tribals, do not make this mask;

11. *Ekadas*—Is a single headed mask either made up of wood or paper masche.

12. *Duvadas*—Is a two headed mask, usually made up of wood;

13. *Zakati Thati*—A bamboo background having few soldiers. Zakti meaning small, bamboo masks having few figures of soldiers;

14. *Vithoba*—Also known as vithal is a male Hindu deity;

15. *Rukhamani*—A female hindu deity, usually shown with vithal. Both vithal and Rukmani are found in a place called Pandharpur in south Maharashtra;

16. *Vetal*—An evial forest spirit;

17. *Gajasur*—Long faced Ganesh;

18. *Evana*—Is a mythological character;

19. *Dhavolaba*—A male god with white face and body. He is a spirit of the forest;

20. *Ghoda*—The spirit of Horse;

21. *Niloba*—God with blue face and blue body;

22. *Mahalaxmi*—The Hindu deity the goddess of wealth worshipped on the second day of Diwali. To the tribals, she is a tribal goddess whose temple is situated in Dahanu;

23. *Shivaji Maharaj*—A Maratha King who worked with the tribals during the Mughal rule. He was instumental in gaining freedom for Maharashtra. The tribals workship him during Bohada;

24. *Masa*—Is yet another character displayed during Bohada. Masa means fish. Tribals occassionally fish but are regularly consumers of dry fish. Since fish forms an important part of their diet, it may have been given godly status;

25. *Surya Dev*—Wooden masks, of Sun are displayed in Nasik during Bohada;

26. *Chandra Dev*—Wooden mask of moon displayed in Nasik, during Bohada.

Analysis of Mask Characters

In all, there are 54 mask characters enacted by the koknas, Thakars, Warlis, Mahadev Kolis, Katkaris, Malhar Kolis, Dhor Kolis etc. of Thane and Nasik districts in the state of Maharashtra. After analysis all the characters we have come to conclusion that the Koknas and Mahadev Kolis who are economically, socially, educationally and politically are better of have a lot of Hindu characters in Bohada clebrated by .them. There two tribes being cultivators have been interacting with the Hindus for long and hence have in corporated characters from Ramayana and Mahabharata in their pantheon.

While the Warlis, Thakars, Katkaris, Malhar Kolis, Dhor Kolis etc. who are socially, educationally, economically and politically quite backward have lot of tribal deities, cosmic forces, forest spirits etc in their Bohada masks. This reveals the socio-economic hierarchy among the tribals, as well as their capacity to celebrate 'Bohada' in a grand or less flashy styles.

Keeping mask characters in the village has multiple advantages They are:

1. The belief that gods are with us provides them moral, mental, and spiritual support;

2. That the presence of these deities facilitates good omen for productive magic such as good rains, good crops, people's welfare etc;

3. This is the best cultural method of preserving the tradition of 'Bohada' and more importantly the making of masks and the techniques these of;

4. Mask festival fetches the villagers money by two ways:

   (a) In giving out masks on hire to another village to clebrate Bohada.

   (b) Collecting taxes from traders who come to sell their goods in the village, during Bohada.

The artist also makes money in the process. Especially when villagers from other villages order new masks or repair the old ones. Thus, the festival of Bohada is celebrated to bring good fortunes to the village by appearing the mask characters.

The Department of Tribal Development and the Ministry of Human Resource Development must encourage such villages so as to preserve, promote and propagate the declining traditions of tribal art. In Bharsatmet we would certainly like to give credit to two families. One Ramchandra Pandhari Nath Bharsat and the second family is of the village head. Currently Laxman Pandu Bharsat is the village head of Bharsatmet.

He has taken maximum interest along with Ramchandra—the mask maker, to organize Bohadas in their village for last 40 years. The Bohada, we witnessed was 38th Bohada organized by these two men. The entire village however supports them. Given below is the case study of Laxman Pandu Bharsat.

CASE STUDY

Personal Background

Laxman Pandu Barsat, a member of Kokna, tribe resident of Bharsatmet village, of Jamsar panchayat in Jawhar block of Thane district, is a head of his village. As the head of the village he has been a pioneer

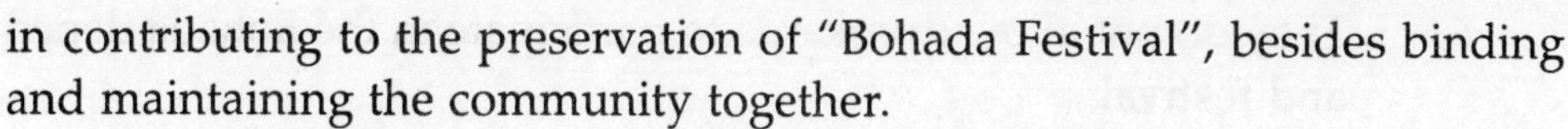

in contributing to the preservation of "Bohada Festival", besides binding and maintaining the community together.

Course of Events

His great grandfather Ramji Patil, who lived almost 300 years ago was an important force in bringing the people of Bharstmet together, so as to preserve the "cult of Bohada" Ramji was in close contact with the king and princess of Jawhar. The king and his royal family belonged to the Mahadev Tribal community popularly known as "Muknes". The king had special interest in Bharsatmet and even other villages of Jawhar celebrating the Mask Festival.

Since Bharsatmet was a village of artists like Ramchandra and Pandurang Bharsat, who were unique, the king of Jawhar may have taken special interest in this village. These and many other factors make the Bohada of Bharsatmet interesting. We have provided an analysis of why we think Bharsatmet Bohada is unique.

Uniqueness of Bohada in Bharsatmet

1. All characters who use traditional masks in Bharsatmet, make new clothes, depending on the character they are palying.
2. Every clan, which has been playing a particular character is responsible for the santity and maintenance of the mask. This includes expenses for clothes as well.
3. The whole village, thereby is involved (Kokna tribe only) in playing these characters.
4. The Head of the village and the Mask Maker's families have to play a key role in organising the Bohada festival.
5. Manachi pati (The Basket of honour) consisting of ten coconuts to be offered to dieties (Masks) comes from the village head's place. Head is designated traditionally as 'patil'.

6. They do not allow drunkards to participate in the Bohada dance and festival.

7. Buisnessman who came to sell different things/commodities in the festival for 3 days have to pay tax to the village. Thus, a sum of Rs. 1000 to 1500 Rs is collected.

8. Every clan which owns a mask pay Rs. 100 to 150 for the festival

9. Besides this, other villagers also contribute money. Thus, a sum of Rs. 10,000 to 15,000 is collected to host the show.

10. They repaint the masks every year.

11. The characters mentioned in this chapter nearly 30 to 35 of them are taken in a procession. Tribals worship them. Some villages display 52 to 54 characters, they also include other Hindu deities common to all the villages, that celebrate Bohada festival is the display of goddess "Jagdamba" or "Ambadevi" on the third day. For the first two days either 30 or 54 characters are displayed in a procession.

On the third day after the family members of the village head and artist bathe, some where at 9 a.m. they bring out the mask of Jagdamba—a female goddess and her procession is taken out nearly for 4 hours for 'darshan'—tribals from other villages offer sacrifices of fowls and goats, including coconuts. This procession is called "Motha Bohada's, because on this day the main goddess is taken into a procession. The Bohada of first two days is called 'Lahan' Bohada. Motha meaning big and Lahan-meaning small. By 4 p.m. in the evening of the third day, Bohada rituals get over.

Worship of Village Goddess

Seven days before Bohada festival tribals in and around Bharsatmet grow cereals such as rice, millets, etc. in a small basket and keep it in a

cool and moist place. By the second day of Bohada there seedlings become six to seven inches. These seedlings are taken in a procession along with musicians to the village goddess (Gaon devi) and offered to her. This ritual in which all the tribal women participate, offer coconut to gaondevi and thank her for foodgrains. Bohada thus, is an expression of gratitude not only to the gaon devi, but all the gods and goddesses, that are displayed and worshipped in the form of mask characters.

12. One of the most interesting aspect of masks of tribals in Thane and Nasik region is the inclusion of hindu gods and goddesses. This is certainly an impact of acculturation. Secondly Mukne Kings who were exposed to modern and urban world played an important role in incorporating certain mask characters, in the process of hinduization.

Myths Associated with Masks of Bharsatmet

Our analysis of the data collected through interviews and observation revealed that two types of myths are associated with "Bohada Festival".

1. Recreation of Ramayan and Mahabharata

Tribals through Bohada try to recreate few scenes of Ramayan and Mahabharat. Besides this they also depict important hindu deities associated with creation of universe. This is however done in a tribal way with their limitation.

2. Tribal Concept of Creation and Cosmos

Most of the mask characters depict tribal concept of creation, cosmos and their perceptions about the same.

In doing so the older generations reminds the younger generation of the knowledge of myths which is transmitted socially to them by word of mouth, that is oral tradition.

The Cult of Bohada: An Institution in Itself

The cult of Bohada is an institution in itself, because it is a platform to socialize and enculturate the younger generation about religion, art, dance forms, music, social relations, rituals, myths, history, drama, seasonal cycle, social solidarity and so on. It enhances organizational ability of the village and promotes cultural and multi-enthnic solidarity. It is a social force that binds and brings people together. Given below is a flow diagram that demonstrates the same.

From the flow chart given below it is evident that the cult of Bohada Festival Cross cuts other domains of tribal life. It is a platform for enriching the process of enculturation and socialization for the younger tribal generations. In the Bohada mask festival youngsters learn:

(i) all about mask characters, their nature and role in sustaining humanity. The powers possessed by these mask gods and goddesses.

(ii) they learn all the processes and sequences of rituals.

(iii) study myths associated with masks

(iv) learn to organize the festival.

(v) enhance their ability to interact and co-ordinate with other tribal and non-tribal communities.

(vi) learn to built up their acting, singing and dancing talents.

(vii) the Bohada festival teaches them to know more about seasonal cycles and economic organizations.

(viii) to stregnthen social relationships.

(ix) to stregnthen social solidarity with in the village, their community and with other communities.

(x) to stregnthen the need to preserve and promote their traditional art forms.

(xi) finally, the cult of Bohada speaks of their cultural heritage, as it is an institution is itself.

CULT OF BOHADA: AN INSTITUTION

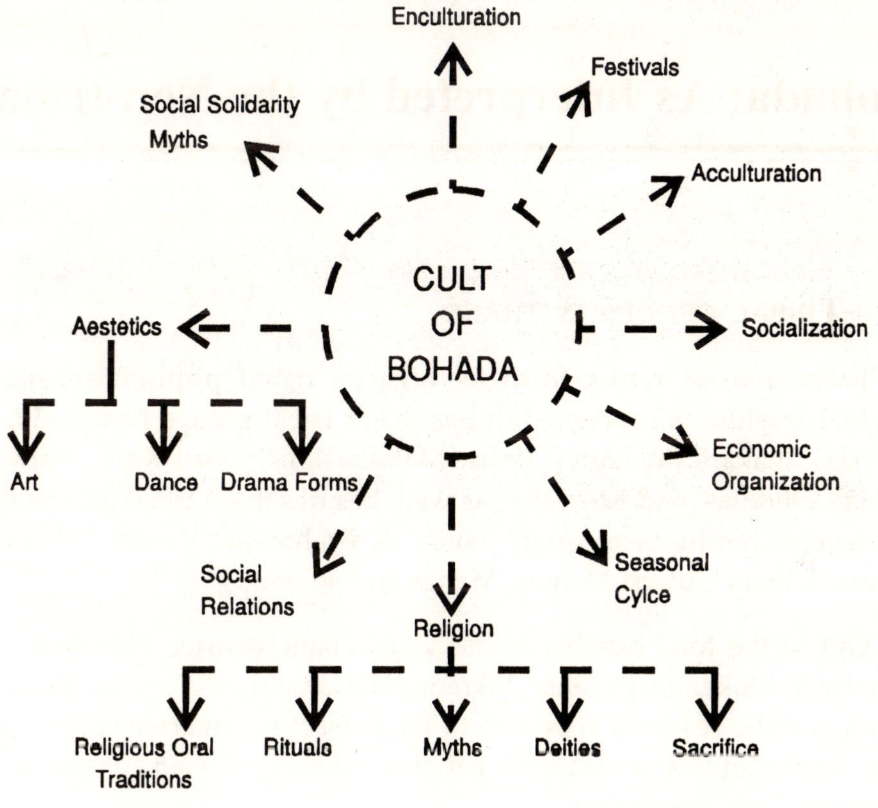

Bohada: As Interpreted by the Non-tribals

Non-Tribal groups in Thane

Thana district ranks third as regards tribal population size in Maharashtra is concerned. It has major tribal groups namely Warlis, Koknas, Thakars, Mahadev Kolis, Malhar Kolis, Dhar Kolis, KatKaris, Dublas, Dhodias, and Kotwalias as well. Besides these tribal groups there are several hindu caste groups such as Brahmans, Kunbis, Marathas, Sonars, Lohars, Sutars, Mahars, Mangs and so on.

Out of the total number of blocks of Thane district, Bohada is very popular in Mokhada, Jawahar, Vikramgod, Dahanu, and part of Shahapur. As a wholistic research approach to the subject we interviewed the non-tribal communities in order to get their view of Bohada Festival. The responses were interesting.

Mokhada: The the birth place of Bohada

Most of them felt that the cult of Bohada was born in the block of Mokhada, 28 kms away from Jawhar. According to Krushna Ram Chandra Dingore, a member of Shimpi (Tailor) caste group aged 72, who has been stitching clothes for Bohada festival for last 60 years states that Bohada was started by his great grandfather late Shri Mukund Ambadas Dingore, who migrated to Mokhada from Nasik in 1857. Mukund migrated to Mokhada because his village Gangapur caught fire. He settled in Mokhad, started his cloth and tailoring business. After few years he established a group in the village which comprised of people from both tribal and non-tribal communities. He was responsible for starting Bohada in Mokhada, block, of the Thane district.

His objective in starting Bohada was to remind people about the 10 incarnations of Vishnu (Dashavtar). According to Hindu mythology Vishnu took several forms to save the earth, humanity and the injustice done to people on the earth by natural and supernatural forces. Mukund Dingore had this in mind, when he first launched Bohada in Mokhada.

Initially there were only ten characters or forms of Vishnu, which were displayed in a procession. Later on these characters doubled to number nineteen. These 19 characters displayed in Mokhada Bohada by majority of non-tribal groups are:

1.	Ganesh—	Played	by	a	Brahman
2.	Saraswati—	"	"	"	Shimpi
3.	Maruti—	"	"	"	Vanjari
4.	Raktadevi—	"	"	"	Warli tribal
5.	Kachha (Tortoise)—	"	"	"	Brahman
6.	Machha (Fish)—	"	"	"	Brahman
7.	Warah (wild Bore)—	"	"	"	Shimpi
8.	Nar sivha (Lion)—	"	"	"	Shimpi
9.	Narad (Man)—	"	"	"	Brahman
10.	Virbadra (Male deity)—	"	"	"	Slimpi

(Contd... .)

11.	Tripurya (Trinity)—	"	"	"	Slimpi
12.	Khanderao—	"	"	"	Brahman
13.	Krishna and Kauravas—	"	"	"	Brahman Marathas
14.	Mhahishasur—	"	"	"	Warli
15.	Londhya—	"	"	"	Warli
16.	Mohini—	"	"	"	Teli
17.	Bhim—	"	"	"	Shimpi
18.	Bakasur—	"	"	"	Mahar
19.	Ram, Laxman, Sita—	"	"	"	Shimpi
20.	Jagdamba—	"	"	"	Shimpi

Even today Mokhada does not display more than 19 to 20 characters. Where as the tribals have increased the number to 52, well, this is what the non-tribals say. Musicians who participate in Mokhada Bohada belong to the Mahar community.

What is interesting about the Bohada of Mokhada is that Jagdamba, who is the oncarnations of Parvati and who kills Mahashasur, the demon, belongs to the tailor caste group. The Shuimpis of Jawhar and Mokhada say that the goddess is their clan deity. Her masks, which is nearly 350 years old has been preserved by Mukund, Dingore and handed over to seven generation after him is currently preserved and worshipped by Jairam Chumble—a Shimpi by caste.

Current status of Bohada in Mokhada

In the year 1948, a registered trust was formed to manage the festival of Bohada in Mokhada. This organization still exists and has been managing the festival professionally. It is said that nearly 50 bags of coconuts are offered to 'Jagdamba'—the main goddess during the festival.

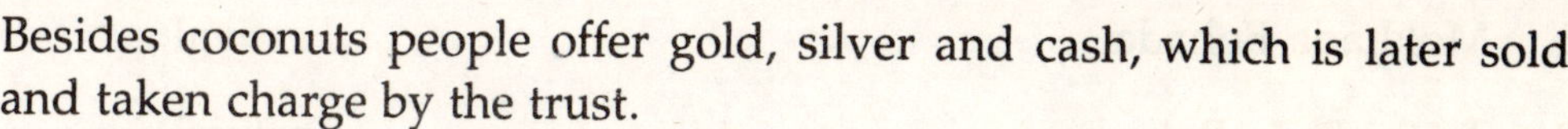

Besides coconuts people offer gold, silver and cash, which is later sold and taken charge by the trust.

Contribution of the Shimpi caste

Besides mask makers, the tailor caste, has contributed to a great deal in preserving and promoting the Bohada festival. Since 1857, begining with Mukund Dingore upto Krushna Ramchandra Dingore a 72 year old tailor the service of stitching garments for Bohada actors has been a significant contribution.

In the entire tahsil of Jawhar only Krushna Ram Chandra Dingore Stitches traditional costumes for the actors of Bohada. He too was a tailor of the Mukne (Mahadev Koli) tribal King of Jawhar. Krushna is 72 years old, owns a shop in Jawhar and lends out traditional costumes of Bohada to tribals and non-tribals, on rent.

He takes a minimum fee of Rs 51/- per garment. Krushna makes traditional caps worn by the tribal kings then. He has four sons namely Madan, Ganesh Sunil and Anil. Except Sunil, no one learnt to stitch traditional costumes. They want to learn how to stitch shirt, pant, blouses, skirts, jackets and other modern clothes.

Krushna feels bad about this. He says I have continued the tradition of stitching Bohada garments for last 60 years of his life. He says his was the seventh generation to do so. I can see the sun of this traditional art setting forever. With my death, the job may die a natural death.

As authors we were lucky to have met Krushna. The information he gave was valuable. We admire the services his family has lent for seven generations, to preserve and promote Bohada.

Villages Carrying on Bohada Tradition

According to Krushna Dingore the cult of Bohada was borrwved by tribal and non-tribal villagers from Mokhada. He rates the best Bohada festivals of Thane as follows:

1.	Mokhada Bohada	Festival
2.	Tarthi Pada Bohada	Festival
3.	Khardi village in shahapur	Festival
4.	Bharsatmet in Jawhar	Festival
5.	Khambala village Bohada	Festival
6.	Dengachimet Bohada	Festival
7.	Nahala Bohada	Festival
8.	Kakda Bohada	Festival
9.	Chalatwad Bohada	Festival
10.	Kara village of Talawali	Festival
11.	Vaishet Bohada and	Festival
12.	Jawhar Bohada	Festival

To conclude this chapter presents view point of the Hindus. Bohada traditionally means a procession. This festival was given birth to by the "Shimpi" (tailor caste) in Mokhada. The founder of the same was a Shimpi, by the name Mukund Ambadas Dingore. Thus, from Mokhada in the year 1857, Bohada was borrowed by tribal and non-tribal villages and interpreted it in their own way. The fact however remains that the participant actors in the festival comprise of both tribals and non-tribals, if we look at Thane and Nasik districts as a whole. However, there are villages, where the scenes are enacted by tribals, only.

Summary and Conclusions

Summary

The present study was carried out to understand tribal masks and myths. The target area of research was Thane and Nasik Districts. Efforts have been made by the authors to throw light on the holistic understanding of Bohada—The Mask festival as a social institution. Interpretations of both tribals as well as non Bribals have been given about the Mask characters.

In order to gather relevant data, mask makers, worshippers, tribal and non-tribals were interviewed. Data was analyzed manually and is presented in six Chapters.

Conclusions

1. The cult of Bohada is a oral history in itself. It was enacted to remind the younger generations about myths, holy events and happenings.

2. Bohada is also looked up as an institution of social control, meaning that the presence of masks in the villages is sought of

creating a terror that gods are with us and we should not deviate from the traditionally designed forms of behaviour.

3. Bohada provides a platform for entertainment to the concerned village and nearby villagers. Meaning there is lot of drinking, eating, dancing romancing which goes on among the spectators who participate in the festival.

4. Bohada has been interpreted differently by the tribals and non-triabls.

5. The makers of Masks as observed were tribals. While the designers of garments were Shimpis.

6. Caste groups such as 'Mahars, Brahmans, Shimpis etc. have played an important role by contributing their services to preserve and promote Bohada.

7. Not to forget the contributions of the Mukne royal family in preserving this cult. It is interesting to note that the Mukne kings belonging to the Mahadev Koli tribe ruled Jawhar for over 700 years. They took keen interest in financially supporting the Bohada cult.

8. It is disheartening to note that master mask makers are hardly 2 to 3 in the entire district of Thane.

9. Both tribal and hindu myths are deeply rooted in the Bohada cult.

10. Tribal masks reveal much more than myths, rituals and stories. Among some tribes of India masks are worn during dances to depict head hunting, marriage ceremonies, fights between good and evil forces, shamanism and so on.

11. The Bohada cult of Thane and Nasik districts very much resembles with the Carnival Festival in Europe.

Where do we go form here?

With rapid modernization and urbanization tribal traditions such as mask cults are fading away. How can these be preserved? Is the question at stake. We feel that these cults can be preserved and promoted by:

(i) **Providing Financial Incentives**: If the villages, wherein Bohadas are popular should be provided with small grants by the Tribal Research and Training Institute and Integrated Tribal Development Projects, of Government of Maharashtra in order to keep the show on.

(ii) **Encourage Mask Makers:** Tribal mask makers should be exposed to urban world to introduce and sell their masks. This would not only fetch them Some money but also have them interested with the urban world;

(iii) **Village Museums:** We believe that Samaj mandirs in the concerned villages should be built to display mask characters. This project should be financed by the Government;

(iv) **Research and Documentation:** There is an urgent need to document these precious cults in the form of written, video, and photo documentation;

(v) **Stipend for elderly and sick Artists:** A stipend of Rs. 300 to 500 per month should be made available to elderly and sick artists.

(vi) **Exposure Abroad:** Efforts should be made to exhibit the mask art to universities and galleries abroad.

Tribal Mask Makers In Maharashtra

We have given below addresses of famous mask makers in Maharashtra.

1. Ramachandra Pandharinath Sonar at Post Bharsatmet, Taluka Jawhar, District Thane. Maharashtra, India.
2. Subhas Dharma Kadu Ram Khind, Sakur Village, Taluka Jawhar, District Thane Maharashtra, India.
3. Sudam Kashinath Bhoye, Ram Khind, Sakur Village, Taluka Jawhar, District Thane Maharashtra, India.
4. Bhagwan Dharma Kadu (same as Above)
5. Sharvan Mulya Gavit, Kali Dhand, Post office Jawhar, Taluka Jawhar, Thane District, Maharashtra, India.
6. Raghunath Babu Budhur, (same as Above)
7. Yashwant Heeru Vatara, Village Pathardi, Post Sakur, Taluka Jawhar, District Thane, Maharashtra India.
8. Krishna Navsu Raut Village Murambi, Post Shirasgaon, Taluka Peth, District Nasik, Maharashtra, India.
9. Jeevram Jeevlya Mahale, Post Borvat, Taluk Peth, District Nasik, Maharashtra, India.
10. Vithal Ravji Limbare, At Post Kohore, Taluka Peth, District Nasik, Maharashtra, India.

REFERENCES

1. Gare G.M. and Sonawane Uttam, Adivasi Kala Vishva, TR and TI, Pune.
2. Jain N.S. and Tribhuwan Robin, 1995, An over view of Tribal Research Studies, TR and TI, Pune.
3. Jain N.S. and Tribhuwan Robin, 1996 Strategies for Promotion and Propagation of Tribal Art, TR and TI, Pune.
4. Jain N.S. and Tribhuwan Robin, 1996 Mirage of Health and Development, Vidya Nidhi Publications, Pune.

5. Tribhuwan Robin and Tribhuwan Preeti, 1999 Tribal Dances of India, Discovery Publishing House, New Delhi.

6. Tribhuwan Robin, 1998 Medical world of Tribals, Discovery Publishing House, New Delhi.

7. Singh C.D. Gare G.M. and Sonawane Uttam, Tribal Handicrafts of Maharashtra, TR and TI, Pune.

8. Census of India, 1961, 1971, 1981 Series 12, Maharashtra, Special tables for Scheduled Tribes.

9. Gare G.M. 2000, Kokna, Inter Continental Publication, Pune.

10. Gare G.M. and Jog Sudhir, 1986, Adivasi Lok Geete, T.R. and TI, Pune.